The Wire Fence Holding Back the World

Martin Willitts Jr

The Wire Fence Holding Back the World

FLOWSTONE PRESS

The Wire Fence Holding Back the World
Copyright © 2016 Martin Willitts Jr.

Winner, 2016 Turtle Island Quarterly Editor's Choice Chapbook Award

Turtle Island Quarterly sponsors the annual Turtle Island Poetry Award. Awards are chosen by the editors. More information available at http://fourdirectionpoetry.wixsite.com/turtleisland

The author would like to thank David Bogue and Jared Smith for selecting this manuscript.

The author gratefully acknowledges the following journals in which these poems appeared previously:

About Place Journal (theme: "Primal Paradox"): "Burying Beetle," "Eastern Tiger Swallowtail Larvae on Black Cherry Tree," "Landslide"
Autumn Sky Poetry Daily: "Barn Swallows," "Symphony #9"
Black Poppy Review: "As Much As Some People Try To Destroy the Earth and All of Its Inhabitants, There Is Still Some Small Hope"
Blue Fifth Review: "Rain"
Broadkill Review: "Bumble Bee"
Homestead Review: "Nearing the End of a Hard Winter," "Storm"
Subprimal Poetry Art: "Snow in the Lost"
Turtle Island Quarterly: "Autumn Clouds," "Chittenango Falls," "Extreme Heat," "Finding a Turtle," "Impossible Weight of Knowing," "Not Only the Extraordinary are Entering the Dream World," "This Hard Winter," "Walking Hill Slopes," "What I Want," "Winter Solstice," "The Wire Fence Holding Back the World"
Verse-Virtual: "Fall," "Hawk Flight before Snowfall," "Song"
"Hedgerow Rose" won 2nd place in the *New York State Fair* poetry contest

First Flowstone Press Edition, December 2016
ISBN-13 978-1-945824-05-0

For Linda Griggs, my wife

Contents

The Wire Fence Holding Back the World	3
Finding a Turtle	4
Extreme Heat	5
Landslide	6
Burying Beetle	7
Bumble Bees	8
Chittenango Falls	9
Walking Hill Slopes	10
Eastern Tiger Swallowtail Larvae on Black Cherry Trees	11
Impossible Weight of Knowing	12
Listening	13
What I Want	14
Hedgerow Rose	16
Barn Swallows	17
Song	18
As Much As Some People Try To Destroy the Earth and All of Its Inhabitants, There Is Still Some Small Hope	19
Symphony #9	20
Storm	21
Rain	22
Autumn Clouds	23
Fall	24
Hawk Flight before Snowfall	25
Winter Solstice	26
Snow in the Lost	27
This Hard Winter	28
Snowstorm Over Independence Pass	29
Nearing the End of a Hard Winter	30
Not Only the Extraordinary are Entering the Dream World	31
Inside Everywhere There Is Light	32

The Wire Fence Holding Back the World

The Wire Fence Holding Back the World

> "I place my feet/with care in such a world"
> — *The Well Rising*, by William Stafford

Light ripples at sunrise
against large dark chunks of breaking night
and the moon folds behind blistered skies
lit by coat-ember light.

Light is wavering
asking to withdraw from hovering this world.
Light drinks from sharp rocks
in purple shadows. Birds crash through sunbreak.

What have I achieved matching this?
I hear pleading long after their flight
curled over the hills, measuring all
who do not listen.

*

Here is where I dig in —
spade breaking soil in intermittent rain
and sun, between gasp and fear,
before this world goes all the way to forgetfulness.

Before harvest and seed fails,
I want this house where trails begin and end,
where light is crystals
and promises are rewarded. Here light comes —

down the hills, touching every leaf
making them hum. My face feels sun
as the ground deepens brown, finds tree stumps,
and voles slinking in wet, uncut grass.

I grip hard on this world. I won't let go —
although, a faraway voice calls to me,
I make the hard decision to stay. Here
light shocks. I cut a barbed wire fence.

Finding a Turtle

I told my son that terrapin shells
hold the secret to Tectonic plates —
he thinks, dinner plates with painted peonies.

The box turtle nudges with flippers
across a stream
of endless stars, like smooth dull stones.

The turtle tugs its prehistoric head in its shell
like a person afraid to admit the truth:
they see the earth plodding to extinction.

My son asks, what if the plates pull apart,
will we fall in the cracks?
He remembers how dinner plates break.

He requests to take the turtle home.
He'd seen one smashed by tires.
I say, it belongs here in the wild.

He considers the fragile peonies,
the stars drowning in silence,
trash piling with nowhere to go.

He suggests the turtle is safer with us.
He dwells on the fissures of life and death.
He demands a turtle shell for a body.

What truth could I give him?
My answers are skid marks.
I crack under pressure.

Extreme Heat

Light penetrates trees into yellow dust,
splitting elements of wind and air.
In this fiery heat, grass becomes raw purple.

This light has a way of contorting trees,
like forging metal. Hot breath.
Whispers inside the light say the storms have left.

The yellow inside the midpoint is white emptiness
where noise is liquefied. It blinds anyone
into deafness. The woods begin moldering.

If you rub a hand across the flat surface
of glass water, it vibrates like these tuning fork trees.
Tones have a way of raising and lowering in pitch.

Like unsettled air and light, in this high frequency,
you never would notice the adjustment,
an owl's wing readying for shifting flight winds.

Landslide

It began with human foolishness.
It began with land erosion.
It began when they cut all the trees.

It rained mountains of rain, washing loose topsoil
like a carpenter uses a plane to smooth surfaces, slices
thin as breath. In the soaked-drenched land, trees unmoored,
sliding down rivulets like strange schooners.
The land was disconnected.

The rain was unable to make up its mind where to go,
what to obliterate. Birds were so saturated,
they could not lift their blue wings.
Water rushed off their tips like rain from roof drains.

The deluge was biblical in proportions.
The rain was the size of carpenter ants.
Muds slid boulders like they were a child's marbles.
Clouds rumbled like an old man clearing his throat.
The land moved like a tsunami,
eradicating every object in its path
like it has been offended by the mere sight.
The behemoth of mud, rain, trees swallowed houses.
The landslide ran out of kinetic energy,
leaving sludge like a giant snail's slime.

Now the assessment begins. Now chainsaws
cut into the truth of what is gone, what remains.
Now there is calling out for the separated and lost.
Now silence claims us
with not one reassuring word to say.
Now there is gathering of brokenness,
the fleshing out of grief into reams of anguish
stretching across continents.

Burying Beetle
    (*Nicrophorus sp*)

There is a dead bird in the woods.
From inside the carcass, a black beetle emerges
with red markings on its forewings.

I forget how we are all hosts to something else.
We all feed; taking in the spirit of the dead
so we can survive, then something feasts on us.

Some say this is ghoulish, but this is life
and death: the recycling of existence.
And it is messy; it is never neat and pretty.

Some say, where is God in all of this?
We want to bury truth, pretend there is more
than larva and decomposition.

We want to compose a reality in stanzas
of lyric beauty, worthy of stature and dignity.
It is impossible. It's not how things work.

They fail to see that this is God's grand design.
And questioning is part of what we do best.
But the dying part — is not what we do best.

Bumble Bees

Ignoring the full-throttle blizzard of bees
crisscrossing around, I try for invisibility.

They are certain as blood in arteries
that the weather will not dip,
and the Echinacea will not lose its aroma.
Their noise is squinting when distant,
buzz saw when near.

I believe in not testing them,
leaving well enough alone.

Bees sound like rusty lawn chairs opening.
They are the lifeblood to the nest, flower,
vegetable, and me. They take shadows
through dizzy-heat and explosions of shade,
moving like Adam's apples in air.
They leave messages at flowers' doorsteps,
then hurtle over fence posts, shimmy corners
like springs uncoiling.

I move under their breath
like a train rolling slowly from final position.

Chittenango Falls

In the dark gravity of these falls
is a muteness of grief
in the air and leaves.

Light passes through its hands.
There are seasons we cannot imagine.
The firm signature of changes comes anyway.
I will not see every day, these changes.
Light is such a giver and taker.
This entire world is built on promises.
And what would happen if nature forgot
to keep those promises? It is quiet, now,
and a kingfisher is the stillness of grass.
All of love is gravity towards the heart.
It is blue and white wings of a kingfisher
rising from water beds of falls and light.
Shadows from leaves turn towards silence.
All weariness jumps out of our bodies.
Light from leaves is fire wanting love.

Walking Hill Slopes

I walk up hill slopes
of layered pine needles
to hear the snap through fall-dip

to focus on what is essential
what I can forget
the humming wind

twisting branches
like feeling the fibers of a feather
I am home

away from the sour-stench city
I can dream this is reality everywhere
sometimes I do not want to turn back

I want to shed my skin like pine needles
when I get like this
I remember why I come back here

and go back there
how can I appreciate what I have
without knowing the difference

Eastern Tiger Swallowtail Larvae on Black Cherry Tree

Survival is always precarious. Every part is connected,
or else parts disconnect, and multiple life forms fail.
Many things can go wrong in life, and they often do.

A male tiger swallowtail with
orange and blue spots near its tail,
traces an indirect route to a milkweed near the vacant road.
Survival depends on feasting and hosting.
Female tiger swallowtails will lay their eggs
on Black Cherry leaves, because
it's the furthest place from their natural enemies.
Survival depends on good choices.

When the eggs hatch, the larva looks like bird droppings.
This camouflage will protect them more than prayer,
more than luck, more than distance and closeness
to their enemies. Survival depends on camouflage.

As the caterpillars grow, they turn green as a Black Cherry leaf,
responding to that deep calling of survival,
a song in their green bloodstream.

There is a resting stage when transformation begins
in greenish-brown chrysalis, small as a thumb.
And if the weather is unexpectedly cold,
the butterfly might wait for spring to emerge.
Those bright eyespots on their wings are not true eyes.
They are illusions to scare their predators
or make the predators to attack the wrong part.
Survival depends on patience.

Survival is always adaptability.
The Easter Tiger Swallowtail can lose a wing
and still survive.

It is we who are the fragile ones.

What will you do to survive?
Will it be the indirect way?
Will you know for certain the best choices?
Survival is always precarious.

The Impossible Weight of Knowing

The boulders decided by themselves to move.
They shed wings of heavy moss,
belying shadows of hawk voices,
abandoning those rivers forgetting their own intentions.

The boulders decided, in tantrum, to move.
Like ballerinas, leaving leased lives,
entering places they did not belong after longing for it so long.
No one knows what they were thinking.

The boulders released themselves from their obligations.
Doors to their hearts opened.
If we gave ourselves to this shredding belief,
what torment to reality would be humbled into joy?

Listening

There was this pull, music
leaning with a sweat-darkened hand,
staring blankly with the grief of a mountain.

When this pull happened,
it carried madness in curled palms,
delicate as a baby's first scream.

This was the sound I heard then: a name
rippling like a sunflower in rain and wind.
It was not a name of anyone I knew.

What was I supposed to do with this information?
It meant nothing to me. Yet, the name
drilled below the surface of memory.

What I Want

I want the kind of morning that lasts
well beyond the everlasting glimmers
and brushes against your body like strung beads
used as a curtain in the entrance to your heart.
These beads should clatter
sounding ever so very much like sleet on hard surfaces.

I want the kind of preserved peace my father felt
after working so hard, seemingly getting nowhere,
as he went deep into the cave of silence
like a hermit crab goes into a larger shell.
His inward spiral would find the edges
towards a center, where nothing could disturb,
a quiet that contemplates. This peace
would fill the stretched-out face of the morning.

I want the diamond-faceted eyes of a bee
seeing everything all at once, everywhere.
I do not want to miss seeing anything.
Those eyes would not blink or flinch
from horror, but would see it for itself —
the disturbance of peace, the rendering of it,
the mute silence afterwards
when everyone realizes how bad it was.

This peace would be a different peace —
more of shock and shame. We would wonder
if reconciliation was possible,
hoping we drained ourselves enough
to be sensible about peace.

I want my eyes see the changing heart
in the sun as it knows peace and silence.

What I want is not unreasonable.
What I want is not impractical.
What I want is not unattainable.
What I want is what all people want —

the silence that is common and essential;
the silence that flourishes;
the silence that rolls loose as a pebble
under the feet of someone climbing towards peace.

I want the silence that will become surrogate stories
we can tell generations, proud of our accomplishments,
stories filling a basket with sunbeams.

Sometimes, things just open up.
Like the sun emerging from a conch shell,
or mountain growing out of your palm
because your breath is the stillness of cranes.
When you speak, bees sting the wicked
with forgiveness, or beads like a rosary
click on your eyes silently when you search
for the peace our fathers never found
while grinding their teeth at the moon.

You asked me what I would want
for my grandchildren. What came to me
was thunder, and silence between
when lightning strikes. How you can count it
to figure out how close it is. How the flash
lasts inside your eyes, even when you close them.
How when lightning stitches across the sky
to ground, it is like an old treadle sewing machine
that does not have a back-stitch. How the rain
has different ways of falling and different sounds,
and how it dictates the length of the rainfall.

How my father would walk in rain to feel it
against his face like sandpaper
to know what God wanted from him.
How his pacing was slow regardless of the rain,
like the rain could not salve whatever was within him.
How the silence was not enough. How drenched
his eyes flash-flooded
until he could barely see where he was going
and could care less when he would come back.
How the bees never stung him.
How stitched we are together.
How nothing is the same when we find the Sublime.

Hedgerow Rose

A miniature hedgerow rose is a drop of purple blood
with injury-finding thorns. These are risks
for persistent todays. Like choices of love,
these trembling intricacies are heard sighing.
It can have all the cool red of strawberries
or robins bopping on the ground of love.
All winter, we wished for shared blades of color.
When the wind chimes vibrate in red suns,
we leave the separateness of love. When rain
showers are flames of movement, let it be
the rose petals of my love. When the days throb
as a headache, let the ripening of roses be heard
calling to remind you how much there is love,
and how it pierces like thorns. When was the last time
you were this lean without love? When sadness
plummeted stars as snowflakes obliterating light?
Or the last time the ground softened like a heart?
Why not release small joys as buds on a rosebush?
You know recovery is around the corner
when the doorbell rings, and it's your lover
kissing like hundreds of red petals on your neck.

Barn Swallows

Under the bare branches shaking their last leaves,
increments of light never reach here.
Two barn swallows are soundless in miles of heat.
They are where the river once cut across.

Not from the church choir,
they are too parched to practice.
They have folded wings into starched clothes
like prayer hands etched from plowing.

They begin gliding for no reason.
Maybe they are trying to stir the stilled air.
Maybe this is why the miles are soundless,
why singing just doesn't help anymore.

Song

A meadowlark flicks songs like wavering candlelight
and infinity is filled

loneliness cannot look back at me
all shadows on leaves vanish

all wars should stop
but do not.

As Much As Some People Try To Destroy the Earth and All of Its Inhabitants, There Is Still Some Small Hope

Many shadows go to the edge of a sheer drop-off
and never jump.
I always approach the mysterious as a lover does.

The troubling is always quiet, like a stone soaking heat.
I am not at home with the easy way about life.
One has to lift those heat-stones now and then,
feel their heft, look for traces of fossils or rattlesnakes.

As the few in power try to eradicate all wildness,
they do not notice the deep well
of interconnected and interdependent species
and how it might lead to their eventual downfall eventually,
and how it is an increasing countdown.

There is such a thing as too much timid caution —
it's not good for you. In this high heat, shadows undulate
and flow, like blue honeysuckles on vines. Time
has its own pace as if it was a whisper of tomorrow.
It does not do any good to be impatient for stars to appear.
Soon there will be too many to count.

Symphony #9

Yes, the sparrows sing in the rain
because they adore the unattainable.
They welcome harshness coming afterwards
when the temperature either dips down
or increases, by ten degrees of misery.
Sparrows sing because joy is misery's twin
and they recognize both like feathers
with or without rain. They sing from branches,
hidden like all great secrets are hidden
and must be searched vigorously.
Their white throats know only release of music
and profound love. They understand music
is given to those who profess. And if they fail,
it is because life had failed them, or if rain
was not long enough, short as pinfeathers.
Rain is giving them what they need. The air
is a great provider. The sky tells: *change comes
and goes*. Smack of rain is decisive song choices.
To the un-listening ear, there is no difference
between before, during, or after rain,
but I have heard the high chattering
and the calm later. I heard the grateful urges
like crocus opening like an aria. I have heard
worms moving out of the soil as ground swells
with rain, and the excitement of sparrows
to see what has been delivered in exchange
for their unsolicited praise. Yes, it rains
birdsongs. Yes, the sparrows flock in numbers
singing *Ode To Joy*. Yes, said Beethoven,
*that is exactly what God wants from us and
how God rewards us*, as his deaf ears filled
with white feathery rainwater. This is how I feel
waking up next to my wife each morning.

Storm

Heavy branches ruffle against the wind
but the dogwood does not want to lose its flower.
It clings to it hard and fast.
Some petals shatter on the ground,
and the world finds more ways to die.

Clouds of flies darken over a dead woodchuck
like the moment before thunder breaks.
It is the same as opening the door to a stranger;
not everywhere do we get a warning.

Death can be slow as a leaky faucet;
but when the sky turns granite color,
soon the world will break apart into pebbles.
Then, how strangely strong will be death's appetite.
There will be a red shadow in the sky.

All we will find afterwards
will be remnants of white dogwood petals.

Rain

*

When rain considers the inner and
outer parts of the silence it makes
as well as the singularity of the moment

all judgment of beauty is from such hunger
it is inevitable to sustain contemplation
it is brushstrokes inside a heart

each distinctive breath or particles of light
or rain droplets on folds of flower petals
or cast-aside watering can or dog nosing a tree

ink dripping on a page
moments of clarity
two worlds never joining

*

slow rain on the underside of a branch
before releasing from stillness
into soft noises of recovery

fifteen different silences
before
and after

world washed and scrubbed
birds sampling a puddle
plucking the music of new life

Autumn Clouds
> Painting by Eric Sloane
> "the sky was created for pure beholding" — Eric Sloane

Over thirty different variations of blue
as a storm gangs-up
ready to double-down on dropping
hail or retribution

temperature changes the white-wash barn
faded grey-blue
as a grizzled old man's unshaven chin
and blisters the paint like worn knuckles

weather-beaten to a pulp
down for the count
taken one to many upper-cut blows
the hill grass flattens powder-blue

the shortness of breath
is in the stacked hay bales
like blue-faced sugar cubes
the hard-set winds stir harsh and icy

slat shutters rattle-clack
weather-vane shifts its weight
gates curve with low-pressure
autumn is bending the rules

Fall

In Fall, asters wither and spiral petals down.
The hot season dwindles towards quiet hours.
Air is more brittle, weather reports more useless.

Night uses a rag to polish the full harvest moon.
Crickets go silent, turning their back on the world.
The over-heated days are over.

Men wearing bright orange hunting vests
enter the woods communally to weed
the overgrown deer population.

Their rifles and shotguns point down like dousers
searching for deer spore. They could care less
if it's out of season. Impatience chills the air.

Hawk Flight before Snowfall

Downhill from the jutted chins of outcrop rocks,
weather rubs its troubled hands of snow.
The ground heaves stone-cold breaths.
Snow grinds every breath into determined movement.

A memory of a hawk is on a weather-beaten fence:
its slightest movements, its sharp, intense focus.
Those same whitewashed, cracked crossbeams
strain against loss.

Turbulent silence takes absence with it.
A hawk is strike and snatch.
Shadows and breath flies out of a heart,
gone before snow or judgment.

If I have lived only this long in the empting wind,
then silence with its message can have its own deepness.
Disappearance finds its way, opening wings of fall.
Swiftness is hardly moving.

Knowledge ends at the door step buried under snow.
What in this uncertain world can be counted on?
I have buried more friends. It's my turn
to be snatched by forthcoming wingless breath.

Winter Solstice

The shortest day in the year, the one where darkness
walked towards school and the only light was snow,
the land wondered if the sun would return,
and it turned its empty trees trying to open the night.
All the animals had been gorging food in preparation,
for these were the famine months. Everyone would forget
the sun and despair. The long hungry shadows were
everywhere.
These were the days before refrigeration, when ice
in the river would be stored for summer on straw.
This is when it was important to have a root cellar,
or cold storage, and we knew how to can. This is when bulbs
slept, dreaming of the future, while we asked about spring.
We would be assured it would be back. It was comforting.
This was before polar vortexes became common. This
was before we tried to shorten the life of the planet.
This was before we heard that weather was opposite
on the other side of the world, and it made no sense.
Now, nothing makes any sense. Too many disbelieve.
The animals and plants and trees are confused.
What we are doing to the planet makes less sense.

Snow in the Lost

allow for shortness of breath
trudging through fields
and fields of endless snow

there is such quietness
you can feel noise
miles away

I have had my share of snow
and on these isolated walks
days are remote blankness

hear that amazing stillness inside
silence is the tiniest sound
sometimes from within

in the brokenness
we all need some point where/when we suddenly notice
the world around us

we find what we've been searching for
has all along
been here in the *Forever*

we all come from these useless whispering miles
wandering in the lost
attracted to what is nameless and felt

and here it is
snow
in the closed-knit trees chewing bird songs

we are bees maddened by too many flowers
in the unnerved sun
where solitude and oblivion are the same

This Hard Winter

This hard winter, the horses' water buckets froze.
I had to chip the ice so they would have something
to drink.

I suppose the horses heard me nearing,
stomping in waist-high snow. It is hard to move
this way. It slows things to almost a stand-still.

It was like the time the tractor was weighed down
in mud, no traction could move it,
like waking a person from a deep sleep.

It was ground deep, like neuropathy,
needing a bigger tractor to pull it,
come spring.

I suppose my eyes were burnt-out
from blinding, reflected snow-light.
I suppose I looked like oblivion.

I was soundless having heard more snow
was heading this way, predicted
to last all week, endless unwanted presents.

I had already forgotten the blue jay
as it settled on a branch before leaving
declaring how wonderful he was, singing.

When I opened the barn door, I had an ice pick.
I looked definitely stranger.
The woods were blotted out by snow behind me.

If you saw the violence when I used the pick,
light swings arc, smoke from my nostrils,
you'd wonder if there was any calm left in the world.

You'd wonder if violence hangs on wooden clothespins.
You'd think all that held sanity together could fall apart,
like a hemlock branch holding too much weight.

Snowstorm Over Independence Pass
        Based on a painting by Russell Chatham, 1998

what is more inconsolable than snow
trying to re-shape the landscape
into its own image

impermanence denies snow from gathering
every time

snow flurries vaporize on sight
like memory or immortality

all traces of footprints
are covered up
like evidence at a crime scene
until there is no proof
we existed

        *

all life is a measurement of forgetfulness
and is silenced

if we make it through this pass
we might make it through
vanishing light
disappearing into *the Beyond*

we will be a blur
caught in a sudden snowstorm
like the Ponderosa
is indistinguishable from the edge
of mountain
silence and death

the return is the need to live

Nearing the End of a Hard Winter

Those first green sprouts — I live for them —
peas curling out of earth coaxing the sun —

however, the air is licking its wounds
from the rough handed-winter, its bruises showing —

how many good days are left?
Many refuse to believe healing flows both ways.

All this waiting is almost torturous. I glance
at the seed packet for delphinium for reassurance.

Not Only the Extraordinary are Entering the Dream World
> "… but others not less extraordinary who step/lightly in to the dream life, refusing to leave" — Jim Harrison, *Returning to Earth*

we come to the dream world
as a tormented river blistering with dead fish

we traveled a doubt-filled pebble lane
recanting every step and this
is where it has taken us

taken is the perfect word for what has happened

we were yanked out of place
from the life we had ignored
to a place where you cannot avoid what you see
and you keep promising
this is not real

it is real and tangible
and we cheapen it by our presence

all love reaches a certain velocity
like a tree split perfectly in half by lightning
or like a bird losing flight
when colliding on a clear window
or when milkweed sending seeds wherever they can go

we came to this dream world all splintery
with our dark and forbidding edges

hundreds of pigeons fled into the uncertain sunset

there is precision everywhere
dead bodies rise and float into endless space
lighter than daylight or a feather

Inside Everywhere There Is Light
> "And we can't see it but we think there's a light inside/
> everything" — William Stafford, *Report to Someone*

There will be a day
when we won't be able to explain anything —

an interval of light from the junipers;
a red aura from a cliff; flecks
of hair on our wrist
finding a pattern of lilac from a cold sun;
the miniature lives owned by rust —

find that intimate glare before it is too late,
tell me what it looks like:
does it glow over tracts of land; or,
does it recede and hide? I have to know
if light is in every place, every tree sap,
every river resolved to be better, every
traveler resting on the roadside
holding a sign telling us where he wants to go
knowing we will never take him all the way.

Every hand letting go of a seed
and the seed itself have light; outside
that last light of day peers over the edge
to see where it is going next.

About the Author

Martin Willitts Jr. is a retired librarian living in Syracuse, New York. He is a visual artist of Victorian and Chinese paper cutouts. He is the author of 10 full-length collections and more than 20 chapbooks. Recent books include *Searching for What is Not There* (Hiraeth Press, 2013), *God Is Not Amused with What You Are Doing in Her Name* (Aldrich Press, 2015), and *How to Be Silent* (FutureCycle Press, 2016). He has won numerous awards, including the 2014 Dylan Thomas International Poetry Award, the 2013 Wild Earth Poetry Prize, and *Big River Poetry Review*'s 2012 William K. Hathaway Award.

www.ingramcontent.com/pod-product-compliance
Lightning Source LLC
Chambersburg PA
CBHW070044070426
42449CB00012BA/3157